The Reactive Manifesto

The Art of Asynchronous Programming

Table of Contents

Chapter 1. Introduction

Navigating the complex world of programming can at times feel like traversing an intricate labyrinth. One emerging area that's reshaping the design landscape is asynchronous programming, brilliantly conceptualized in the "Reactive Manifesto." This Special Report, in a comforting and approachable manner, unpacks this highly technical topic, aiming to make it accessible to developers at all experience levels. Within these pages, we delve deep into this manifesto's principles, exploring its beauty through real-world implementation examples and presenting its potential impact on the future of software design. We assure you, this concise yet comprehensive report will be a valuable addition to your programming toolkit, whether you're simply curious or actively practicing asynchronous programming. Don't miss an opportunity to be at the forefront of this significant shift in programming practice.

Chapter 2. Understanding the Reactive Manifesto

The Reactive Manifesto, conceived in 2013, is a fundamental document that helps to conceptualize complex asynchronous programming ideas into four core principles that simplify software development process: Responsive, Resilient, Elastic, and Message Driven. These principles enable developers to build systems that can effectively handle growing demands in a scalable, flexible, and fault-tolerant manner, while maintaining end-user satisfaction as a top priority.

2.1. The Importance of Being Responsive

The foremost principle in the Reactive Manifesto is responsiveness, which essentially implies that the system should respond in a timely manner, under all circumstances. A responsive system is essential to retain credibility in the face of users. If a system is slow to respond, users may consider it faulty or unsuitable for their needs.

The concept of responsiveness pivots around two core aspects: latency and predictability. Latency refers to the delay between making a request and receiving a response. Lower latency values are usually desirable since they denote faster response times. Predictability, on the other hand, involves consistent system behaviour over time. Systems with high predictability have lesser instances of erratic behaviour, which aids user satisfaction.

Latency reduction and predictability increase can be achieved via efficient resource utilization, load balancing, and partitioning, among other strategies.

2.2. Building Blocks for Resilience

A resilient system gracefully manages failures without impacting user experience. Based on the principle of resilience, systems should function continuously, despite the presence of component failures. This requires the ability to restore full functionality swiftly while continuing to respond to requests.

The central concept here is 'supervision,' where parent components manage child components. If a child component fails, the parent can handle the failure by restarting, stopping, or replacing the child, ensuring the system remains functional and that the failed component does not impact other parts of the system.

Software systems comprising loosely coupled components can isolate and contain failure in distinct areas, preventing cascading failures. The supervisor model supports this isolation approach, making resilience a core characteristic of reactive systems.

2.3. The Elastic Aspect

The third principle, elasticity, is about the system's capacity to expand and contract according to demand. An elastic system can manage a variance in workload efficiently, by dynamically allocating and deallocating resources. This adaptive capability can significantly cut down operating costs while ensuring optimal user experience under varied load conditions.

Implementing elasticity involves employing strategies like horizontal scaling (adding or removing servers), vertical scaling (increasing or decreasing server resources), or a combination of both. It's underpinned by automatic provisioning and de-provisioning strategies to handle load fluctuations effectively.

Elasticity embodies the feedback loop principle. Observations about a specific condition become the input for making adjustments. By monitoring system performance metrics, automated decisions can be made to scale resources up or down as required.

2.4. A Message-Driven Architecture

The last principle of the Reactive Manifesto calls for system design to be message-driven. Rather than traditional request-response architectures, reactive systems leverage asynchronous messaging for communication, leading to the decoupling of system components. This Non-blocking communication allows recipients to consume messages when they are ready, so processing resources aren't wasted waiting for responses.

Message-driven architecture empowers all the other principles. It supports responsiveness and resiliency through location transparency, as it removes temporal coupling and allows for the supervision of components. Additionally, it enables elasticity via flexible, dynamic routing and load balancing.

Message-driven communication could be implemented using various techniques and technologies, such as event-driven architectures, message queues, or actor models.

2.5. The Cumulative Potential of Reactive Systems

In summary, Reactive programming provides a powerful approach to building highly scalable, resilient software systems. The Reactive Manifesto's four guiding principles form a roadmap for designing and implementing such systems.

By focusing on responsiveness, resilience, elasticity, and a message-driven architecture, we create an asynchronous system that balances load, manages failure, and maintains low latency, all while adapting to changing demand. It is thus an approach that anticipals and embraces the dynamic, asynchronous nature of modern software development, making it an indispensable tool in the programmer's toolbox.

Understanding and effectively applying the principles of the Reactive Manifesto can significantly enhance the way we design and build efficient, scalable, and user-friendly software systems for an ever-evolving digital world.

Chapter 3. The Art of Asynchrony: Simplified

Let's begin our exploration of the art of asynchrony, understanding the nuances of its form and function, and delve into its implications for software design to make it both intuitive and effective.

3.1. Understanding Asynchrony

Asynchronous programming, at its most basic form, refers to operations that allow a program to continue executing other instructions while waiting for certain events or tasks to be completed. Fundamentally, it is about doing multiple things potentially at the same time, without having to stop the overall process.

This model is in stark contrast with synchronous programming, where one operation must complete before the next one begins, like a line of people waiting to order coffee. However, with asynchrony, multiple orders can be taken and processed at the same time, more akin to a fast-food restaurant.

Broadly speaking, the advantage of asynchronous programming is performance. It allows more efficient usage of resources since a single thread can handle multiple requests or tasks. There's no idle time, the wheels of computation and instruction fulfilling keep turning, which leads to potentially faster, more responsive applications.

It's imperative to note that asynchrony doesn't necessarily mean concurrency or parallelism, even though they often coexist. Concurrency is about dealing with many things at once (which can be achieved via interleaving on single-core machines), while parallelism is about doing many things at once, which usually requires multiple-core machines to fully utilize.

3.2. So, Why Asynchronous?

The demand for highly responsive systems in today's multi-core, distributed system environments has led to the popularization of asynchronous programming paradigms. These paradigms enable systems to handle a significant number of requests concurrently, in a non-blocking and resource-efficient manner.

Developers have grown fond of asynchronous programming because it improves system throughput and maintainability. These two quality attributes are crucial considerations for system performance and future adaptability. Asynchronous systems can scale to handle high load while maintaining responsiveness, making them a reliable solution for developers targeting users requiring instant response from their applications, even under heavy usage.

In today's high-demand service landscape, companies and developers cannot afford the performance degradation common with synchronous programs. Users expect a fluid service, and the non-blocking asynchrony provides the potential to deliver this quality.

3.3. The Challenge with Asynchrony and Reactive Programming

Undeniably, asynchrony brings a set of challenges. One key challenge is the significant shift in mindset required to write and understand asynchronous code. Unlike the straightforward, top-to-bottom flow of synchronous programming, asynchronous design patterns can often involve more complex control flows, making the code harder to reason about and debug.

Reactive programming is a remedy for managing this growing complexity. As defined by the Reactive Manifesto, reactive software development is an approach to building systems that are more robust, responsive, and flexible. It is designed to handle the "message-driven" nature of asynchronous systems gracefully.

The Reactive Manifesto emphasizes four key traits: responsiveness, resilience, elasticity, and message-driven architecture. These traits co-op to provide a seamless application operation, even under various challenging environmental conditions.

3.4. Asynchrony in Practice: JavaScript Promises

One of the most explicit illustrations of asynchronous programming is JavaScript's Promise object. A Promise in JavaScript represents an operation that hasn't completed yet but is expected in the future. It is an assurance that there will be a result in due course.

JavaScript Promises are the perfect representation of asynchronous operations. They serve as a return value from an operation that'll be realized in the future. With Promises, JavaScript allows for operations to be chained together using .then() and errors can be caught with .catch(), supplying an elegant, handleable layout for asynchronous programming.

A Promise is in one of these states:

- pending: initial state, neither fulfilled nor rejected
- fulfilled: the operation completed successfully
- rejected: the operation failed

Promises in Javascript reduce the burden of handling asynchrony and make it easier to manage and reason about. This object is fundamental to managing complex, interdependent asynchronous operations in JavaScript.

3.5. Conclusion

The rise of asynchrony marks a shift to reimagine what is possible with programming. The essential takeaway is to view asynchrony as an ally, a powerful tool that allows programmers to run processes independently of each other, improving the efficacy of your programs when handled correctly.

Asynchronous programming, and more broadly, the Reactive Manifesto's principles, herald a new era in programming where the system responsiveness and user experience take the wheel. They significantly alter the design landscape and hint at more revolutionary changes to come as we continue to unravel the possibilities they offer.

Though the understanding and implementation of asynchrony can be complex, it is sure to be a worthwhile investment in your developer toolkit. Don't shy away from the challenge. Embrace the art of asynchrony. The future of programming is unfolding, and it's showing to be brilliantly asynchronous.

Chapter 4. The Principles of Reactive Programming

Asynchronous programming, and specifically, Reactive programming, rely on a few fundamental principles to guide their design and execution. These principles are responsiveness, resiliency, elasticity, and message-driven architecture. Each of them contributes significantly to the design and subsequent efficacy of Reactive systems, forming the backbone of this advanced type of programming.

4.1. Responsiveness

Responsiveness is a cornerstone of Reactive programming. At its most fundamental, a system is responsive if it responds in a timely manner. This principle may seem simple but it comes heavy with implications for the design and operation of the system.

Firstly, a responsive system promotes user engagement and satisfaction, ensuring that system users retain continuity with their tasks. A responsive system delivers results as fast as expected or even faster, contributing to overall positive user experience.

In terms of design, responsiveness implies that system components should prioritize non-blocking operations. This means adopting conflict detection and resolution mechanisms, such as optimistic and pessimistic locking methods and embracing concurrency in all its levels—thread, process, and system-wide.

From an operational standpoint, responsiveness ensures that the system remains fully functional and capable of addressing user demands at all times, irrespective of the load. This not only promotes user satisfaction but also contributes to resource utilization efficiency.

4.2. Resiliency

Resiliency, another principle of Reactive programming, asserts that a system should remain responsive in the face of failure. This contingency-focused rule requires that system designers anticipate possible points of failure and create appropriate contingency plans, sometimes referred to as 'fault tolerance.'

Here, the emphasis is on isolating and managing faults as opposed to eliminating them. Achieving zero fault likelihood is implausible; designing a system that can tolerate and bounce back from faults is, however, a practical and worthwhile pursuit.

Resiliency in reactive systems is often achieved through modularity, the partitioning of the system into multiple independent components or modules. If a module fails, the function of the overall system is not compromised as other modules can pick up the slack. This is often referred to as redundancy in system design.

In essence, a resilient system is designed with backup plan following Murphy's Law - "anything that can go wrong will go wrong." Therefore, when things go wrong, the system isn't completely brought down and it quickly recovers and returns to normal operation.

4.3. Elasticity

Continuing along the principles of Reactive programming, we encounter elasticity. This principle postulates that a system should remain responsive under varying workloads.

Elasticity is about being able to scale in response to the application's demands. For application designers and architects, this means that your application can either scale up, scaling out, or, ideally, both in reaction to an increase or decrease in demand.

An elastic system can allocate and deallocate resources as required, scaling up to meet high demand and then scaling down during periods of less intensity. This capability is usually facilitated by a dynamic pricing model, where resources (like processors and storage) can be allotted and billed based on usage.

In addition to managing and optimizing resource consumption, an elastic system helps maintain responsiveness. As more resources are made available, the system can better ensure timely responses to user requests, even under heavy load.

4.4. Message-Driven Architecture

The last principle of Reactive programming is its message-driven nature. In this architecture, components communicate via messages. This principle is predominantly where the asynchronous nature of Reactive programming comes in: the communication between different parts of the system is not direct, it is achieved by passing messages.

Message-driven design decouples system components, allowing them to evolve independently, promoting both system reliability and scalability. Messages can be passed synchronously or asynchronously, but the preference in Reactive systems is toward asynchronous delivery because of its non-blocking nature.

A message might be a command, stating an action to perform, or an event, representing a state change. When one component wants another to perform an action, it sends a command message. When a component changes state, it sends an event message to all interested parties.

To pull this off successfully, system designers must have effective message-handling strategies in place. Messages must be immutable to prevent modifications mid-transit, which would jeopardize system consistency. They must also have identifiers to enable their tracking and monitoring in the system.

In conclusion, the principles of reactive programming - responsiveness, resiliency, elasticity, and message-driven architecture - promote an efficient, reliable and user-centric system design approach. Exploring and understanding these principles can help not only in grasping the concept of reactive programming but also in applying its principles in real-world software design and development scenarios. Be it an experienced developer or a novice in the field, mastering the principles of reactive programming will equip you with skills and tools to create powerful, robust systems. This will certainly increase your value in the competitive field of software development, opening doors to bigger and exciting opportunities.

Chapter 5. Real-world Scenarios in Asynchronous Programming

In the fascinating universe of programming, asynchronous programming draws an unsettling picture for novices and, quite often, for seasoned programmers. Yet, the Reactive Manifesto has shed new light on this convoluted field by introducing a fresh conceptualization. Now, let's embark upon a memorable journey into real-world applications of asynchronous programming that will give readers a better grasp of this concept through concrete and tangible scenarios.

5.1. Asynchronous Programming in Web Servers

The world of web development provides an excellent starting point for our journey. When a web server begins processing a request, executing it synchronously would block all other requests, leading to performance challenges. Asynchronousism shines here by starting to process the request and immediately freeing up the server to accept and handle other requests.

A real-world example of this would be in the Node.js runtime environment, where developers utilize JavaScript's asynchronous characteristics for non-blocking I/O operations. For instance, file handling or networking can be conducted parallelly, ensuring responsiveness and scalability. Thus, asynchronous programming enables a single-threaded server to handle numerous requests concurrently, preventing the negative impact of potential bottlenecks.

5.2. Databases and Asynchronous Interaction

Databases, the reservoir of information, are another area where asynchrony fanfare can be heard. Queries can be long and demanding, potentially stalling other operations. Consider a situation in a financial firm where the system must execute a time-consuming report generation for one user while not hindering market data updates for others.

Asynchronous calls here ensure that the system can initiate the report generation query while allowing for other operations to proceed. The report data is then gathered when ready, notifying the system and completing the operation. This design both saves time and prevents other operations from freezing during heavy database handling, adding efficiency and maintaining system responsiveness.

5.3. Social Media and Real-time Notifications

Fast-paced social media platforms advocating real-time updates like Facebook, Twitter, or Instagram also embrace async methods. Whenever users post statuses or images, their followers don't need to continually refresh pages to get the updates. Instead, asynchronous programming enables the server to update all followers simultaneously, once posts are ready to publish. These platforms also handle millions of concurrent users without latency, underlining the practicality and efficiency of async operations.

5.4. Asynchronous Programming and APIs

In a globalized world, software integration demands quick and efficient data exchange, making asynchronous programming pivotal in API (Application Programming Interface) development. Python's asyncio library helps manage the asynchronous execution of code, allowing the API to respond to requests by merely initializing tasks and moving to the next ones before the previous tasks finish.

Consider when a system might need to pull data from several APIs concurrently. With synchronous execution, each API call must wait for the previous to complete before initiating, leading to extended overall execution time. But with asynchronous programming, each API call initiates independently and concurrently, thus reducing the total interaction time.

5.5. Microservices and Asynchronous Communication

Last but not least, we delve into the distributed world of microservices, where services communicate over a network. Synchronous communication can introduce tight coupling and set back services waiting for others to respond. Asynchronous communication flows, using techniques like event-driven architecture or message queues, solve this issue. For instance, when an Order service needs to inform an Inventory service about a new order, it sends a message and continues with its other tasks. The Inventory service picks this up when ready, hence promoting loose coupling and allowing services to operate at their own pace.

From web servers to APIs, asynchronous programming is deeply insinuated into the software fabric, playing a pivotal role in serving the highly concurrent and real-time nature of today's digital interactions. By embracing asynchronous coding practices, developers can bridge the gap between what software needs to do and what resources it has to do it, enhancing promptness, scalability, and efficiency in the complex labyrinth of concurrent programming. However, this coin's other side warns about the risks of callback hell, race conditions, and deadlocks. Thankfully, many modern programming languages are adopting async/await syntax to manage these challenges elegantly and efficiently, solidifying async programming as a powerful tool in a programmer's arsenal.

Chapter 6. Building Resilient Software: A Reactive Approach

In accordance with the "Reactive Manifesto," building resilient software necessitates a shift in approach to software development. This chapter will guide you on this journey, focusing on key principles and real-world implementations that typify a truly reactive system design.

In your role as a developer, architect or designer, understanding the tenets of reactive design is paramount. This chapter will provide a comprehensive overview that will empower you with the knowledge and tools required to appreciate and implement resilient software using a reactive approach.

6.1. The Principles of Resilience

Resilience, as defined by the "Reactive Manifesto," is fundamentally the system's ability to bounce back from calamities. It signifies the system's knack to stay responsive even during adversity. The principle of resilience is rooted in three main concepts: redundancy, isolation, and delegation.

Redundancy implies having backups in place and ready to take over when a part of the system fails. This ensures service continuity and prevents the propagation of failure.

Isolation presupposes that components of the system live in isolation such that a failure in one component does not directly result in the failure of others. This property is mostly achieved through mechanisms like data encapsulation and asynchronous message passing.

Delegation pertains to assigning the role of error handling to external components, making sure that the failing system is not burdened by its own recovery, thus ensuring that the system remains responsive despite internal failures.

6.2. Embracing Failure as a First-Class Citizen

In traditional software development, developers aim to prevent failures. In contrast, reactive software design encourages the recognition of failure as a first-class citizen. Failures are inevitable in any system; the reactive approach argues for designing the system in such a way that it can deal with failures effectively, rather than simply striving to prevent them.

Error kernel, a core architectural pattern of resilience, may be employed to ensure that failures are contained within each component and do not propagate to disrupt the system's health and functioning. The kernel contains the components that must stay healthy for the system to remain responsive. The integrity of these components is continuously monitored and protected so that the system can remain flexible and resilient.

6.3. Resilience through Architectural Design

Let's discuss a real-world example that showcases resilience through architectural design. Consider designing a microservice-based application for an e-commerce business. This kind of architecture would involve multiple services, such as inventory, user management, payment, and order management among others.

In a reactive approach, these services would be designed to be isolated, ensuring that a fault in one service doesn't propagate to the others. They communicate asynchronously and have managed redundancies. For instance, the payment service, a critical service for the business, could have multiple instances running concurrently to cater to high loads and potential failures. This ensures that the entire system remains available and responsive, even if one part of the system experiences failures.

6.4. The Role of Software Tools in Building Resilient Systems

Building resilient software is not just about embracing the principles discussed above; it's also about using the right tools for the job. Languages like Scala and frameworks such as Akka, Play, and Lagom, have been specifically designed to adhere to the principles of reactive programming. They promote asynchronous operations, resilience, and high concurrency levels.

Specifically, Akka, an open-source toolkit and runtime, facilitates building highly concurrent, distributed, and fault-tolerant event-driven applications on the JVM. With built-in modules for clustering, persistence, and testing among others, it aids developers in creating applications that are resistant to failure and capable of self-healing.

6.5. Conclusion

In striving for resilient software design, the "Reactive Manifesto" illuminates a path forward, situating resilience firmly at the center of system designing. Redundancy, isolation, and delegation are key principles driving resilience, with several software tools available to aid developers in realizing these principles within their applications.

Embracing failures, using the right architectural patterns, and picking the right programming language and frameworks, will collectively lead you to the wonderland of resilient software. This journey, while potentially challenging, is also immensely rewarding, enabling the creation of responsive, resilient, and elastic systems that freely embrace the ebb and flow of change and failure.

Embrace this future, become Cognizant of the inherent benefits, and build software that remains responsive in the face of adversity, gracefully managing failures as a routine part of doing business in our complex and interconnected digital world.

Chapter 7. Scalable Architectures: Embracing Asynchrony

We initiate this exploration by understanding the nature of traditional synchronous systems and why scalability contributes to their limitations.

Modern software systems, especially those based on a microservices architecture, are inherently distributed. Users are spread across different geographical time-zones and interact with systems through various devices and networks. Data is stored and processed concurrently on multiple machines to ensure high availability and the ability to handle increasing load.

The distributed nature and growing complexity of these systems has challenged the synchronous or blocking model of building software. With synchronous systems, the application thread that triggers an operation must wait for that operation to complete before it can continue. While waiting, this thread is not available to perform other tasks. With a growing number of users and operations, the amount of wasted computational resources due to idle threads increases, creating a scalability bottleneck.

Implementing asynchronous strategies can address these challenges.

7.1. Embracing Asynchrony

Asynchronous programming is not a new concept; however, it is gaining attention due to its effectiveness in handling the inherent concurrency and latency in modern distributed systems.

In the asynchronous model, operations can run concurrently without blocking the application thread. Since operations are not tied to particular threads, more operations can be initiated concurrently, and threads can serve more requests. This non-blocking nature of asynchronous programming allows for better resource utilization, improved scalability, and the ability to handle spikes in load.

7.2. The Event-Driven Paradigm

To realize the benefits of asynchrony, one must adopt the event-driven paradigm. An event-driven system reacts to events like user actions, system events or messages from other programs. These events are often handled non-sequentially, meaning the flow of program is not dictated by the sequence of events.

In an event-driven system, a central unit receives and dispatches events to handlers that take care of processing the event. These handlers run asynchronously and possibly in parallel, which can optimize resource use and performance of the system.

7.3. Real-World Examples

Let's take the example of a movie recommendation system. When a user comments on a movie, it triggers an event. The system, instead of immediately updating the user's recommendation list, places this event in a queue. An event handler processes the event when resources are available, updating the recommendation list asynchronously and ensuring that the user can continue to interact with the system, unhindered by the recommendation update operation.

7.4. Reactive Manifesto Principles Applied

The Reactive Manifesto describes both needed attributes for scalable architectures (Responsive, Resilient, Elastic, and Message-Driven) and characteristics of a system to stay responsive in case of failure (Resilient by design) and under varying load (Elastic).

These principles can be applied for scalable architectures through asynchrony. By embracing asynchrony, systems can strive towards the principles of the Reactive Manifesto.

7.5. Message-Driven

Adopting a message-driven architecture inherently creates a system that supports asynchronous communication. Each component is isolated, communicates via bounded messages, and stays ignorant of the senders or recipients of such messages. It opens up the possibility of decentralization, adding another level of scalability.

7.6. Resilience

Asynchrony also aids resilience. Non-blocking interactions ensure continued operation in the face of component failures. For instance, if a service fails, it does not prevent the system or its users from performing other tasks due to locked resources.

7.7. Elasticity

Elasticity is the ability to scale up or down according to workload changes. Asynchrony enhances the elasticity of a system. By allowing threads to be free, it enables the system to scale and handle an increase in workload efficiently.

7.8. Conclusion

In conclusion, Embracing Asynchrony brings significant advantages for designing scalable architectures. It enhances resource utilization, improves performance, and accommodates the increasingly concurrent nature of modern software.

Adopting principles from the Reactive Manifesto, asynchronous programming offers a tried and tested path to creating more responsive, resilient, and elastic systems, paving the way for software of the future.

Chapter 8. Revisiting Design Patterns through a Reactive Lens

Modern software engineering's landscape is continually evolving, with new paradigms often disrupting the status quo. Asynchronous programming, expressed elegantly through the Reactive Manifesto, is one such invention, providing developers with a powerful set of principles and methodologies. From traditional design patterns, we are shifting towards designs more efficient in handling async or non-blocking tasks—embracing what is known as reactive design patterns.

8.1. The Basics of Reactive Programming

Before we delve into how reactive programming influences design patterns, we need to grasp the basics of reactive programming itself. It is an asynchronous programming paradigm oriented around data streams and the propagation of change, with an emphasis on scalability, resilience, and responsiveness.

With reactive programming, we think in terms of data flowing through our application, responding to changes across the system, enabling a higher degree of flexibility and control. Developers can write nondeterministic programs in a declarative manner, controlling the interaction rules among entities rather than specifying each interaction.

8.2. Reimagining Traditional Design Patterns

Design patterns – solid, reusable solutions to common software problems – provide a critical vocabulary for developers. Still, with the rise of reactive programming, we must revisit these patterns with the reactive lens.

Let's consider a few common design patterns:

1. Singleton: This pattern restricts a class from instantiating multiple objects. Consider doing this reactively; the Singleton object functions as a response to system demand, the object is instantiated first time it is required and reused again from then onwards.

2. Observer: In this model, objects (observers) react to an event from an observed object, establishing a one-to-many dependency. A reactive implementation could involve a data stream as an observable, with subscribers (observers) reacting to changes in the data stream.

3. Builder: The Builder pattern abstracts the steps involved to create an object. In the reactive paradigm, the individual creation steps could be replaced with data streams, responding reactively to changes.

8.3. Embracing Reactive Design Patterns

Now, let's acquaint ourselves with some reactive design patterns:

1. Back Pressure: In a system where data producers and consumers have mismatched processing rates, the faster element needs to accommodate the slower one to prevent overload. Back Pressure

pattern handles such scenarios, allowing the slower party to control the data flow.

2. Message-Driven Architecture: This pattern delivers messages (events) to recipients asynchronously, decoupling the sender and receiver temporally and spatially.

3. Circuit Breaker: This pattern is used to detect failures and encapsulates logic to prevent a component from continually trying to execute a particular operation that might fail.

8.4. Marrying Reactive Patterns with Systems Design

While theory is essential, applying reactive patterns effectively in real-world systems is the ultimate goal. Let's consider a simple example: designing a high-volume concurrent system for an eCommerce platform.

The key aspects of our design would need to capitalize on the strengths of reactive programming – asynchronous processing, strong isolation, event-driven execution, and decentralized control. We can leverage Message-Driven Architecture to handle hundreds of thousands of concurrent user requests. On top of this, a Back Pressure pattern can maintain system reliability by controlling data flow and preventing system overloads. For system-level protection, the Circuit Breaker pattern can prevent cascading failures.

8.5. Exploring the Future with Reactive Patterns

The influence of reactive programming on design patterns is growing. Today, reactive patterns are helping its developers manage the asynchronous nature of modern systems, tackling the challenges across domains. Yet, we've only begun exploring the depth and breadth of the reactive universe, with its profound impact on future software development.

By revisiting and reimagining traditional design patterns through a reactive lens, we can push the boundaries of system design and architecture. As we look forward to another era of software engineering, this exploration brings both promise and challenge, but with the potential of redefining how we design and build software in a highly connected, asynchronous world.

We have only scratched the surface of the implications of applying the principles of the Reactive Manifesto to our design patterns. The journey to full reactive system design is a transformative process., where each step forward impacts every layer of your development process. Despite its initial complexity, unlocking the promise of reactive systems may herald the next leap forward in efficient, resilient, and responsive software design.

As we navigate the intricacies of modern programming together, remember that reactive programming isn't merely a shift in technique; it is a shift in perspective. By viewing our software designs through a reactive lens, we can approach the labyrinthine world of programming with endurance, innovation, and anticipation of the potential that awaits us at every turn.

Chapter 9. The Impact of The Reactive Manifesto on Modern Software

In 2013, a small group of developers came together to pen a document that would, in the years to come, dramatically reshape our understanding of modern software development. The "Reactive Manifesto" articulated a set of principles intended to guide developers towards building more robust, efficient, and flexible software. As we've since discovered, this Manifesto has become an enduring frame of reference within the world of asynchronous programming, inspiring numerous libraries, frameworks, tools, and methodologies in its wake.

9.1. Behind The Reactive Manifesto

It would be amiss to discuss the impact of the Reactive Manifesto without first elaborating on the conditions that led to its inception. The group of developers behind the Manifesto, including Jonas Bonér, Viktor Klang, Roland Kuhn, and Martin Thompson, were at that time grappling with the challenges posed by the increasing ubiquity of multicore processors, distributed computing architectures, and Big Data technologies. To meet these challenges head-on, they conceived a need for a new software architecture design approach.

The Reactive Manifesto laid out four fundamental principles. It proposed that systems should be Responsive, maintaining responsiveness under all conditions. Resilience, the ability to recover from failures rapidly, became another essential tenet. They focused on Elasticity, the ability to scale up or down as needed. Finally, systems should be Message-Driven, centering around non-blocking communication.

9.2. Shift in Programming Paradigms

The significant shifts in the programming paradigm brought about by the Reactive Manifesto cannot be overstated. Traditional development models primarily hinged upon the request-response pattern of synchronous communication. This approach, while intuitive to human understanding, could introduce performance bottlenecks and posed complications in distributed environments. The propagation of The Manifesto heralded an attitudinal shift towards asynchronous, message-driven architectures, better equipped to handle volatile workloads and failures in a distributed environment.

Reactive programming represents a significant departure from seemingly instinctive synchronous development patterns towards more sophisticated asynchronous, non-blocking patterns. Asynchronous execution, while complex in terms of controlling flow and managing errors, offers substantial benefits, including improved system resource utilization, higher throughput, and enhanced experience for users. The Manifesto has been instrumental in encouraging developers to venture into this intricate yet rewarding space.

9.3. Influence on Libraries, Frameworks, and Tools

An important measure of the Reactive Manifesto's impact is the wide range of libraries, frameworks, and tools that have adopted its principles. From Java's Project Reactor and Spring WebFlux, to JavaScript's RxJS, to the .NET world's Reactive Extensions, a myriad of libraries and frameworks revolve around these ideas.

Perhaps the most widespread embodiment of the principles of the

Reactive Manifesto is the Reactive Streams initiative. Conceived to provide a standard for asynchronous stream processing with non-blocking backpressure, Reactive Streams brought together industry giants like Netflix, Lightbend, Pivotal, Red Hat, and Twitter. The Reactive Streams initiative resulted in the inclusion of the `java.util.concurrent.Flow` API in Java 9, cementing the concepts of the Manifesto in arguably the most widely used programming language.

9.4. Potential Impact On Future Software Design

Looking towards the future, it's clear that the influence of the Reactive Manifesto continues to grow. The horizontal scaling offered by reactive systems is particularly suited to the developing trends of cloud computing and Microservices architecture, where the ability to adapt to fluctuating load conditions is key.

Moreover, technologies and trends like IoT (Internet of Things), Big Data, AI, and even edge computing are amplifying the need for software that is resilient, responsive, and scalable, which are exactly the principles the Reactive Manifesto promotes. The Internet of Things, for instance, presents an environment of vastly distributed devices with unpredictable workloads and failures, calling for the applications of Reactive Systems.

Another indication of the continued impact of the Reactive Manifesto is the increasing adoption of reactive programming in both front-end and back-end development. JavaScript developers, with libraries such as RxJS or frameworks like Vue or Angular, equally reap the benefits of the reactive approach, and it's percolating into mainstream app development.

In summary, the Reactive Manifesto, with its cohesive set of principles and strong focus on meeting the practical challenges of modern software design, has left an indelible imprint on the world of programming. Its impact resonates through numerous libraries, frameworks, and tools and continues to shape our forecasts for future software paradigms. As both source of inspiration and a guiding light, the Reactive Manifesto will continue to shape the future of asynchronous programming as we navigate through this exciting period of evolution in software design.

Chapter 10. Beyond The Reactive Manifesto: The Future of Asynchronous Programming

Understanding the Reactive Manifesto is only the beginning of our journey in the realm of asynchronous programming. Its principles provide a solid foundation upon which we can build robust, reactive systems. However, to envision a future where these principles are ingrained in the fabric of software development demands a deeper exploration. Here, we stand at the precipice of this fascinating journey, equipped with the insights we have gleaned from the manifesto, eager to delve into the potential impact of this shift and its tangible manifestations in real-world scenarios.

10.1. A Look at Current Trends

As technology evolves at a breakneck pace, so does our demand for more efficient and performant systems. Be it the high-frequency trading systems of Wall Street or video streaming services like Netflix, the need for responsive, scalable, human-centric architectures is more acute than ever. Asynchronous programming techniques, as delineated in the Reactive Manifesto, are proving to be vital solutions to meet these growing demands.

function task1() { ... return result_of_task1; }

function task2() { ... return result_of_task2; }

const result1 = task1(); const result2 = task2(); [/code]

In the synchronous code snippet above, task2() waits until task1()

completes. If task1() takes a long time, it keeps task2() waiting, reducing efficiency and performance.

Compare this with asynchronous code:

function task1() { return new Promise((resolve, reject) ⇒ { ... resolve(result_of_task1); }); }

function task2() { return new Promise((resolve, reject) ⇒ { ... resolve(result_of_task2); }); }

Promise.all([task1(), task2()]) .then(results ⇒ { // Handle results of both successfully completed tasks }) .catch(error ⇒ { // Handle error }); [/code]

In this version, task1() and task2() run simultaneously, improving efficiency. This is just a simple utilization of the asynchronous programming concepts codified in the Reactive Manifesto.

10.2. Evolution of Programming Paradigms

Beyond just responding to changing demands, asynchronous programming also reflects a fundamental shift in our programming paradigms. Procedural, object-oriented, and functional programming have each had their day in the sun, addressing the prevailing concerns of their respective eras. Reacting to the complexities of our current digital landscape, the industry is shifting toward more asynchronous, event-driven approaches.

The history of programming paradigms is a feedback loop. Developers create software to solve problems; they encounter difficulties; to address these, they devise new programming paradigms. The inception of the Reactive Manifesto and the subsequent rise of asynchronous programming is a perfect example of this loop.

10.3. The Role of Language and Framework Support

The evolution and adoption of a new programming paradigm also depend heavily on language and framework support. Luckily, major languages like Java, JavaScript, Python, and C# have embraced this shift and are introducing constructs to make asynchronous programming more natural and intuitive. Key software frameworks like Akka, Spring Reactor, and Vert.x are offering powerful tools for creating reactive systems.

JavaScript's evolution, in particular, is noteworthy. Being the language of the web, its advancement significantly influences the global developer landscape. With the introduction of Promises, Generators, and the elegant async/await syntax, JavaScript has made it easier for developers to write and reason about async code.

```
async function getTodos() { try { const response = await
fetch('https://jsonplaceholder.typicode.com/todos'); const todos =
await response.json(); console.log(todos); } catch (error) {
console.error(error); } } [/code]
```

Above is an example of async/await syntax in JavaScript. Instead of callback hell, we have linear, easy-to-understand code that handles asynchronicity gracefully. It's examples like these that strengthen the case for a future dominated by asynchronous programming.

10.4. GraalVM: Unifying Languages and Tools

While individual languages are doing their part to incorporate asynchronous programming, GraalVM goes a step further. This universal virtual machine allows running programs written in various languages – JavaScript, Python, Ruby, R, JVM-based languages, and even WebAssembly – within the same application.

Such technological advancements aid the adoption of asynchronous programming paradigms. By unifying multiple languages and offering tools that support asynchronous constructs, GraalVM is playing a significant role in shaping the future of programming.

10.5. Into the Future: Quantum Computing

As we explore the future trajectories of asynchronous programming, it's worth considering the potential impact of quantum computing. The probabilistic nature of quantum bits (qubits) places a tangible emphasis on the need for asynchronous programming methods. As we get closer to building feasible quantum computers, it will be interesting to see how the principles outlined in the Reactive Manifesto help shape this emerging field.

In conclusion, the Reactive Manifesto has served as a spark, kickstarting a meaningful conversation about our current programming practices. Asynchronous programming, with its focus on creating robust, human-centric systems, is no longer just an alternative; it's quickly becoming the norm. Through this exploration, it's abundantly clear that our journey into a future dominated by asynchronous programming is not merely a matter of choice but a necessity ordained by the complex challenges of our time.

Chapter 11. Implementing Reactive Principles: A Project Guide

Firstly, it's crucial to understand that the Reactive Manifesto defines four principles that govern a reactive system: Responsive, Resilient, Elastic, and Message-Driven. This chapter highlights how to practically implement these principles using a hypothetical project scenario.

11.1. Understanding the Components of a Reactive System

A reactive system comprises several interoperating components that synchronize through message-passing. A primary characteristic of this system is non-blocking communication, fostering responsiveness and elasticity.

When designing a project based on the Reactive Manifesto, it's useful to start by identifying component interactions. Traditionally, in a synchronous system, components directly invoke each other's methods. In contrast, a reactive system uses asynchronous message-passing, thereby freeing up resources for other tasks during waiting times.

For example, imagine a restaurant application where each component symbolizes a role, such as customer, waiter, chef, etc. Rather than having the waiter stand idle while the chef prepares the meals – synchronous behavior – the Reactive Manifesto proposes the waiter serves other guests – asynchronous behavior.

11.2. Building Responsiveness into the System

The Reactive Manifesto stipulates that a responsive system should respond promptly, providing quick feedback. The system's design must prioritize responsive user interfaces, monitoring, and system management.

Suppose we are using our restaurant application during peak hours. The business requires the system to maintain a high level of performance despite the increased load. To realize this, the system might implement a load balancer to distribute tasks and ensure rapid response times.

Remember, the goal of a responsive system is not to guarantee the fastest possible execution time, but rather predictability. This ensures that users know what to expect and can plan accordingly.

11.3. Incorporating System Resilience

Another key element of our Reactive application is its resilience, the ability to handle failures gracefully and heal itself. This implies coordinating error handling among different system components.

Suppose a chef falls ill in our restaurant scenario, the system should ensure that other staff members can take over the chef's responsibilities without compromising service quality.

In practical terms, the application can duplicate critical components, isolate them, and facilitate automatic recovery when they fail. Errors are encapsulated in messages and forwarded to other parts of the system for handling.

Crucially, resilience must be a primary concern from the beginning of development and thoroughly integrated into the system architecture.

11.4. Ensuring System Elasticity

Elasticity refers to a system's ability to scale up or down based on workload, ensuring efficient resource utilization. An elastic system can handle varying workloads by distributing computational tasks across multiple computing cores or networked computers.

In a physical restaurant, elasticity can manifest in adjusting the staff numbers according to the expected customer flow.

For our restaurant application, a load balancer can dynamically add or remove nodes based on traffic. Modern cloud computing services often provide such elastic scaling capabilities, making it easier to implement this principle.

11.5. Promoting a Message-Driven Architecture

The final principle, a message-driven approach, enables non-blocking behavior, providing system decoupling and isolation. This allows system components to maintain autonomy, ensuring that failures or slowdowns in one part don't significantly impact the others.

Translating this to our restaurant scenario, implementing a message-driven system means applying a method where communication (like orders or instructions) pass in messages rather than method calls.

In practical terms, we might use a message queuing system like RabbitMQ or Apache Kafka to organize communication between system components.

The project journey adopting Reactive programming practices can at first feel daunting. However, by understanding and implementing these principles - Responsiveness, Resilience, Elasticity, and Message-Driven design, teams can navigate this new territory confidently. This shift necessitates a certain level of unlearning and relearning, but the result is a system that can leverage modern hardware and infrastructure efficiently, handle failures gracefully and provide a more user-friendly, predictable experience.

This exploration into the Reactive Manifesto and its principles has highlighted the primary characteristics a software system needs to meet the ever-evolving demands of today's digital world. As we delve into specific technologies and libraries that support these principles in subsequent chapters, remember the inherent philosophy underneath them all: creating software that can proficiently react to changes, in a world where change is the only constant.

Redefining your understanding of system design and embracing this shift in thinking can seem like a profound challenge, but it's a transformation that also presents considerable advantages. The journey begins with understanding the deep lines in the Reactive Manifesto, but it extends far beyond that into a new way of viewing software design. Remember, the manifesto isn't prescribing specific solutions, but instead proposing a paradigm shift. This shift, once understood and executed well, has the potential to redefine the software landscape dramatically.

www.ingramcontent.com/pod-product-compliance
Lightning Source LLC
LaVergne TN
LVHW051627050326
832903LV00033B/4692